Spread a Little Joy

© 2010 Kraft Foods except for photography on pages
12, 14, 22, 32, 34, 60, 78, 80, 90, 100, 102, 104, 108, 138, 146, 148, 152
which were reproduced with permission of Louis Petruccelli
of Louis Petruccelli Photography

Published by Kraft Foods. Three Lakes Drive, Northfield, IL 60093

For inquiries regarding this book, contact Kraft Foods Global, Inc.
at 1-800-634-1984

Printed in Italy by NAVA Press

Art direction, layout and design by mcgarrybowen Chicago

PHILADELPHIA and PHILLY are trademarks of Kraft Foods

ISBN 978-0-615-37248-8

Spread a Little Joy

A COLLECTION OF SIMPLE AND DELICIOUS
PHILADELPHIA RECIPES TO INSPIRE AND ENJOY

Table of
contents

08   **Appetizers**

36   **Entrées**

106   **Side Dishes**

130   **Desserts**

158   Handy Tips

160   Index

162   Acknowledgments

The recipes within these pages share one key ingredient: PHILADELPHIA Cream Cheese. From there, the possibilities are limitless.

Pasta gets infused with personality. French toast becomes more magnifique. Veggies get exciting. Eggs start to sing. Even a simple tomato sauce becomes more decadent. Consider PHILLY the beginning of a creamier, more enticing eating experience.

With 70 inspiring recipes, *Spread a Little Joy* lets you create a world of alluring appetizers, exciting entrees and delectable desserts. Each dish is tasty in itself, but we've left plenty of room for creativity and experimentation.

So don't limit yourself. Spread a little joy. Spread a little smile. And start spreading PHILLY to places you never thought possible.

APPETIZERS

Bacon-Cheese Crescents

Preparation time:
20 minutes

Total time:
35 minutes

Makes:
16 servings

1 pkg. (8 oz.) PHILADELPHIA Cream Cheese, softened

8 slices bacon, cooked, crumbled

⅓ cup grated Parmesan cheese

¼ cup finely chopped onions

2 Tbsp. chopped fresh parsley

1 Tbsp. milk

2 cans (8 oz. each) refrigerated crescent dinner rolls

1　HEAT oven to 375°F.

2　MIX all ingredients except crescent dough.

3　SEPARATE each can of dough into 8 triangles; cut each triangle lengthwise in half. Spread each dough triangle with 1 generous tsp. cream cheese mixture. Roll up, starting at short side of triangle. Place, point-side down, on baking sheet.

4　BAKE 12 to 15 min. or until golden brown. Serve warm.

Southwest White Chicken Pizza

Preparation time:
15 minutes

Total time:
27 minutes

Makes:
9 servings

1 refrigerated ready-to-use baked pizza crust (12 inch)

½ cup (½ of 8-oz. tub) PHILADELPHIA Cream Cheese Spread

1 boneless skinless chicken breast (¼ lb.), cooked, sliced

¼ cup slivered red onions

⅓ cup picante sauce

½ small avocado, thinly sliced

1   HEAT oven to 400°F.

2   SPREAD pizza crust with cream cheese spread; top with chicken and onions.

3   BAKE 10 to 12 min. or until crust is golden brown.

4   TOP with remaining ingredients.

TIP
Substitute shredded cooked beef or pork for the chicken.

Tomato and Balsamic Bruschetta

Preparation time:
10 minutes

Total time:
23 minutes

Makes:
16 servings

1 loaf French bread (16 oz.), cut into 16 slices

2 cloves garlic, halved

1 tub (8 oz.) PHILADELPHIA ⅓ Less Fat than Cream Cheese

16 cherry tomatoes, halved

½ cup slivered red onions

2 Tbsp. balsamic vinegar

2 Tbsp. olive oil

1 tsp. brown sugar

⅛ tsp. *each* salt and pepper

¼ cup small fresh basil leaves

1   HEAT oven to 400°F.

2   PLACE bread slices in single layer on baking sheet. Bake 3 to 4 min. on each side or until toasted on both sides. Rub one side of each slice with cut side of garlic. Cool.

3   SPREAD each toast slice with 1 Tbsp. reduced-fat cream cheese; top with tomatoes and onions.

4   WHISK vinegar, oil, sugar, salt and pepper until well blended. Drizzle over toast slices; top with basil.

Baked Triple-Veggie Dip

Preparation time:
15 minutes

Total time:
50 minutes

Makes:
4 ½ cups or
36 servings,
2 Tbsp. each

1 ½ cups grated Parmesan cheese, divided

1 can (1 lb. 3 oz.) asparagus spears, drained, chopped

1 pkg. (10 oz.) frozen chopped spinach, thawed, drained

1 can (8 ½ oz.) artichoke hearts, drained, chopped

1 tub (8 oz.) PHILADELPHIA Chive & Onion Cream Cheese Spread

½ cup mayonnaise

1 HEAT oven to 375°F.

2 MIX 1 ¼ cups Parmesan with all remaining ingredients.

3 SPOON into 2-qt. baking dish; top with remaining Parmesan.

4 BAKE 35 min. or until dip is heated through and top is lightly browned.

Smoked Salmon Chips

Preparation time:
10 minutes

Total time:
10 minutes

Makes:
12 servings

½ cup (½ of 8-oz. tub) PHILADELPHIA Cream Cheese Spread

1 Tbsp. finely chopped fresh chives

1 Tbsp. finely chopped fresh dill

1½ tsp. milk

½ tsp. orange zest

24 kettle-cooked rippled potato chips

1 pkg. (4 oz.) thinly sliced smoked salmon, cut into 24 strips

1 MIX first 5 ingredients until well blended.

2 ARRANGE chips in single layer on platter. Roll each salmon strip into cone shape; place 1 on each chip.

3 TOP with cream cheese mixture. Garnish with additional chopped fresh chives.

Chicken and Corn Quesadillas

Preparation time:
10 minutes

Total time:
25 minutes

Makes:
8 servings

6 oz. cooked boneless skinless chicken breasts,
   cut into thin strips

½ cup frozen corn

½ cup salsa

4 flour tortillas (8 inch)

½ cup (½ of 8-oz. tub) PHILADELPHIA Chive & Onion
   ⅓ Less Fat than Cream Cheese

1   COOK chicken, corn and salsa in skillet on medium heat
    8 to 10 min. or until heated through, stirring occasionally.

2   SPREAD 2 tortillas with reduced-fat cream cheese; top
    with chicken mixture and remaining tortillas.

3   HEAT large skillet sprayed with cooking spray on medium
    heat. Add 1 quesadilla; cook 4 to 5 min. or until golden
    brown on both sides, turning after 2 to 3 min. Repeat with
    remaining quesadilla. Cut into wedges.

TIP
Substitute black beans for
chicken for a vegetarian option.

Squash and Cherry Tomato Quiche Cups

Preparation time:
30 minutes

Total time:
48 minutes

Makes:
12 servings

2 cups chopped butternut squash (½-inch pieces)

2 tsp. olive oil

12 slices white bread, crusts removed

12 cherry tomatoes, halved

½ cup (½ of 8-oz. tub) PHILADELPHIA Cream Cheese Spread

3 eggs

¼ cup whipping cream

2 Tbsp. chopped fresh chives

⅛ tsp. *each* salt and pepper

1 HEAT oven to 400°F.

2 TOSS squash with oil. Spread onto baking sheet. Bake 15 min. or until tender. Meanwhile, flatten bread slices with rolling pin. Press 1 piece onto bottom and up side of each of 12 muffin pan cups sprayed with cooking spray.

3 COMBINE squash and tomatoes; spoon into bread cups. Beat remaining ingredients with whisk until well blended; spoon over squash mixture.

4 BAKE 15 to 18 min. or until centers of filling are set and tops are golden brown.

Creamy Guacamole

Preparation time:
15 minutes

Total time:
15 minutes

Makes:
1½ cups or
12 servings,
2 Tbsp. each

2 fully ripe avocados

¼ cup (¼ of 8-oz. tub) PHILADELPHIA Cream Cheese Spread

¼ cup finely chopped tomatoes

2 Tbsp. finely chopped onions

2 Tbsp. lime juice

1 clove garlic, minced

⅛ tsp. salt

Dash black pepper

1 MASH avocados in medium bowl.

2 ADD remaining ingredients; mix well.

TIP
To ripen an avocado quickly —
store in a paper bag with a
ripe banana at room temperature
until avocado is soft.

Chicken and Cranberry Bites

Preparation time:
10 minutes

Total time:
25 minutes

Makes:
24 servings

1 pkg. (17.25 oz.) frozen puff pastry (2 sheets), thawed

¾ cup (¾ of 8-oz. tub) PHILADELPHIA Cream Cheese Spread

1½ cups chopped cooked chicken breasts

½ cup whole berry cranberry sauce

1   HEAT oven to 425°F.

2   UNFOLD 1 pastry sheet on each of 2 lightly floured baking sheets. Cut each pastry sheet into 12 squares.

3   SPOON 1½ tsp. cream cheese spread onto center of each pastry square. Top with chicken and cranberry sauce.

4   BAKE 14 to 15 min. or until pastry is golden brown, rotating baking sheets after 7 min.

TIP
Use a pizza cutter to easily
cut the pastry dough.

Greek Artichoke Dip

Preparation time:
10 minutes

Total time:
30 minutes

Makes:
3 cups dip or
24 servings,
2 Tbsp. each

1 pkg. (8 oz.) PHILADELPHIA ⅓ Less Fat than Cream Cheese,
  softened

1 can (14 oz.) artichoke hearts, drained, chopped

½ cup shredded Parmesan cheese

2 cloves garlic, minced

1 small red pepper, chopped

1 pkg. (3.5 oz.) crumbled reduced-fat feta cheese

1 Tbsp. sliced black olives

1 HEAT oven to 350°F.

2 MIX first 4 ingredients until well blended.

3 SPOON into 3-cup ovenproof serving dish; top with peppers and feta.

4 BAKE 20 min.; top with olives.

TIP
Serve with pita chips.

Rustic Caramelized Onion Tart

Preparation time:
25 minutes

Total time:
40 minutes

Makes:
12 servings

1 large onion, thinly sliced

8 slices bacon, chopped

1 ready-to-use refrigerated pie crust (½ of 15-oz. pkg.)

1 pkg. (8 oz.) PHILADELPHIA Cream Cheese, softened

¼ cup sour cream

½ cup shredded Swiss cheese

1 COOK onions and bacon in skillet on medium-high heat 10 to 12 min. or until onions are tender, stirring frequently.

2 HEAT oven to 400°F. Unroll pie crust on baking sheet. Mix cream cheese and sour cream; spread onto crust. Spoon onion mixture onto center of crust, leaving 2-inch border. Sprinkle with Swiss cheese. Fold border over filling, leaving opening in center and pleating crust as necessary to fit.

3 BAKE 12 to 15 min. or until crust is lightly browned. Cool slightly.

Asian-Style Chicken and Cashew Cakes

Preparation time:
20 minutes

Total time:
45 minutes

Makes:
15 servings

1 lb. ground chicken breast

1 red onion, finely chopped

4 oz. (½ of 8-oz. pkg.) PHILADELPHIA Cream Cheese, softened

⅓ cup plus 1 Tbsp. cashews, finely chopped, divided

⅓ cup *each* chopped fresh basil and cilantro

Zest of 1 lemon

2 Tbsp. flour

¼ cup oil

¼ cup packed brown sugar

¼ cup white vinegar

¼ cup water

1 Tbsp. chili sauce

2 tsp. fish sauce

1 serrano chile, sliced

15 fresh basil leaves

1 COMBINE chicken, onions, cream cheese, ⅓ cup nuts, herbs and zest. Roll into 15 balls; flatten slightly. Dip in flour, turning to coat both sides of each. Shake off excess flour.

2 HEAT oil in large deep skillet on medium-high heat. Add half the chicken cakes; cook 3 to 4 min. on each side or until done (165°F) and golden brown on both sides. Drain on paper towels. Repeat with remaining chicken cakes; cover to keep warm.

3 MIX next 6 ingredients and remaining nuts in saucepan; cook 3 to 5 min. or until sugar is dissolved and sauce is slightly thickened, stirring frequently.

4 PLACE chicken cakes on basil leaves. Serve with sauce.

Sun-Dried Tomato and Garlic Dip

Preparation time:
5 minutes

Total time:
5 minutes

Makes:
2 cups or
16 servings,
2 Tbsp. each

1 tub (8 oz.) PHILADELPHIA Cream Cheese Spread

½ cup mayonnaise

½ cup sun-dried tomatoes packed in oil, drained, chopped

2 Tbsp. finely chopped fresh chives

1 clove garlic, minced

1 tsp. freshly ground black pepper

1   MIX all the ingredients until well blended.

2   SERVE with crackers and cut-up fresh vegetables.

TIP
For a colorful presentation,
serve dip in hollowed-out
bell peppers.

ENTRÉES

Steak with Creamy Peppercorn Sauce

Preparation time:
10 minutes

Total time:
22 minutes

Makes:
4 servings

1 boneless beef strip steak (1 lb.), well trimmed

2 tsp. olive oil

1 tsp. cornstarch

½ tsp. brown sugar

½ cup beef broth

½ cup (½ of 8-oz. tub) PHILADELPHIA Cream Cheese Spread

2 Tbsp. green peppercorns

1 HEAT grill to medium-high heat.

2 BRUSH both sides of steak with oil. Grill 4 to 6 min. on each side or until medium doneness (160°F). Remove from grill; cover. Let stand 5 min.

3 MEANWHILE, mix cornstarch and sugar with whisk in medium saucepan. Gradually stir in broth; cook on medium heat 2 min. or until thickened, stirring constantly. Add cream cheese spread and peppercorns; cook and stir 2 to 3 min. or until cream cheese is melted and sauce is well blended.

4 SLICE steak. Serve topped with sauce.

Sausage and Peppers Lasagna

Preparation time:
30 minutes

Total time:
1 hour 30 minutes

Makes:
12 servings

½ lb. Italian sausage

1 onion, chopped

½ cup *each* chopped green and red peppers

2 pkg. (8 oz. each) PHILADELPHIA Cream Cheese, softened

½ cup milk

2½ cups shredded mozzarella cheese, divided

½ cup grated Parmesan cheese, divided

1 jar (24 oz.) spaghetti sauce

½ tsp. dried oregano leaves

½ cup water

12 lasagna noodles, cooked

1   HEAT oven to 350°F.

2   BROWN sausage with onions and peppers in large skillet on medium-high heat. Meanwhile, beat cream cheese and milk in medium bowl with mixer until well blended. Combine mozzarella and Parmesan. Reserve 1½ cups. Add remaining to cream cheese mixture; mix well.

3   DRAIN sausage mixture; return to skillet. Stir in spaghetti sauce and oregano. Add ½ cup water to empty sauce jar; cover with lid and shake well. Stir into meat sauce. Spread ⅓ of the meat sauce onto bottom of 13x9-inch baking dish; cover with 3 noodles and half the cream cheese mixture. Top with layers of 3 noodles, half the remaining meat sauce and 3 noodles. Cover with layers of remaining cream cheese mixture, noodles, meat sauce and reserved cheese. Cover with foil sprayed with cooking spray.

4   BAKE 1 hour or until heated through, removing foil after 45 min. Let stand 15 min. before cutting to serve.

Croque Monsieur

Preparation time:
5 minutes

Total time:
5 minutes 30 sec.

Makes:
2 servings

2 slices Italian bread (½ inch thick)

2 Tbsp. PHILADELPHIA Chive & Onion Cream Cheese Spread

2 ham slices (2 oz.)

2 Swiss cheese slices

1   HEAT broiler.

2   PLACE bread on baking sheet. Broil, 3 inches from heat, 30 sec. or until toasted. Turn.

3   SPREAD with cream cheese spread; top with ham and cheese.

4   BROIL 30 sec. or until cheese is melted.

TIP
For a change of pace, prepare using salami and provolone cheese slices.

Trattoria Tortellini

Preparation time:
5 minutes

Total time:
20 minutes

Makes:
6 servings,
1½ cups each

2 pkg. (9 oz. each) refrigerated three-cheese tortellini, uncooked

1 cup milk

4 oz. (½ of 8-oz. pkg.) PHILADELPHIA Cream Cheese, cubed

6 Tbsp. shredded Parmesan cheese

¼ tsp. black pepper

1 pkg. (6 oz.) baby spinach leaves

1 cup quartered cherry tomatoes

1 COOK pasta as directed on package.

2 MEANWHILE, cook milk and cream cheese in large skillet on medium heat until cream cheese is melted and mixture is well blended, stirring occasionally. Stir in Parmesan and pepper. Add spinach; mix well.

3 DRAIN pasta. Add to spinach mixture with tomatoes; mix lightly.

TIP
For a change of pace, add ¼ tsp. crushed red pepper and the zest of 1 lemon to sauce with the Parmesan and black pepper.

Tandoori Chicken Kabobs

Preparation time:
10 minutes

Total time:
50 minutes
(incl. marinating)

Makes:
4 servings

2 oz. (¼ of 8-oz. pkg.) PHILADELPHIA Cream Cheese, softened

2 Tbsp. tandoori paste

1 lb. boneless skinless chicken breasts, cut into 12 pieces

1   MIX cream cheese and tandoori paste in medium bowl. Add chicken; toss to coat. Refrigerate 30 min. to marinate.

2   HEAT broiler. Remove chicken from marinade; reserve marinade. Thread chicken onto 4 skewers; brush with reserved marinade. Place on rack of broiler pan.

3   BROIL, 6 inches from heat, 8 to 10 min. or until chicken is done, turning after 5 min.

TIP
Serve with flavorful cooked rice.

Asparagus and Parmesan Tart

Preparation time:
30 minutes

Total time:
54 minutes

Makes:
8 servings

1 ready-to-use refrigerated pie crust (½ of 15-oz. pkg.)

1 Tbsp. oil

2 onions, thinly sliced, separated into rings

¾ lb. fresh asparagus, trimmed, blanched and cut into
   1-inch lengths

4 oz. (½ of 8-oz. pkg.) PHILADELPHIA Cream Cheese, softened

½ cup sour cream

2 eggs

½ tsp. lemon zest

½ cup shredded Parmesan cheese, divided

1   HEAT oven to 400°F.

2   LINE 9 ½-inch tart pan with removeable bottom with crust; trim edge. Prick bottom with fork. Bake 10 to 12 min. or until lightly browned. Cool.

3   MEANWHILE, heat oil in nonstick skillet on medium heat. Add onions; cook 10 min. or until caramelized, stirring occasionally. Spoon into crust; top with asparagus.

4   BEAT next 4 ingredients with whisk until well blended. Add ¼ cup Parmesan; mix well. Pour over asparagus; top with remaining Parmesan.

5   BAKE 20 to 24 min. or until filling is slightly puffed and set in center.

Grilled Salmon with Creamy Pesto Sauce

Preparation time:
10 minutes

Total time:
20 minutes

Makes:
4 servings

4 salmon fillets (1 lb.)

¼ tsp. *each* salt and pepper

2 Tbsp. olive oil

¼ cup milk

4 oz. (½ of 8-oz. pkg.) PHILADELPHIA ⅓ Less Fat than Cream Cheese, cubed

2 Tbsp. pesto

1 Tbsp. finely chopped fresh parsley

1   HEAT grill to medium heat.

2   BRUSH both sides of fish with oil; sprinkle with salt and pepper. Grill, skin-sides down, 10 min. or until fish flakes easily with fork.

3   MEANWHILE, cook reduced-fat cream cheese and milk in saucepan on medium heat 2 to 3 min. or until cream cheese is completely melted and sauce is well blended, stirring constantly. Stir in pesto.

4   SERVE fish topped with sauce and parsley.

Savory Mushroom Omelet

Preparation time:
5 minutes

Total time:
11 minutes

Makes:
1 serving

1 tsp. olive oil

½ cup sliced fresh mushrooms

2 eggs, beaten

⅛ tsp. freshly ground black pepper

2 Tbsp. PHILADELPHIA Chive & Onion
⅓ Less Fat than Cream Cheese

1 HEAT oil in small nonstick skillet on medium-high heat. Add mushrooms; cook and stir 2 min.

2 ADD eggs and pepper; cook 2 to 3 min. or until eggs are almost set, lifting edge with spatula and tilting skillet to allow uncooked portion to flow underneath. When egg mixture is set but top is still slightly moist, top omelet with small spoonfuls of reduced-fat cream cheese.

3 SLIP spatula underneath omelet, tip skillet to loosen and gently fold omelet in half. Slide or flip omelet onto serving plate.

Creamy Chicken Penne

Preparation time:
15 minutes

Total time:
35 minutes

Makes:
4 servings,
1½ cups each

2 cups penne pasta, uncooked

¾ lb. boneless skinless chicken breasts, cut into thin strips

1 small onion, chopped

1 Tbsp. olive oil

2 cups sugar snap peas

1 small red pepper, chopped

2 tsp. minced garlic

2 Tbsp. butter

1 Tbsp. flour

1½ cups milk

4 oz. (½ of 8-oz. pkg.) PHILADELPHIA Cream Cheese, cubed

½ cup shredded Romano cheese

1 Tbsp. finely chopped fresh parsley

1   COOK pasta as directed on package. Meanwhile, cook chicken and onions in hot oil in large skillet on medium heat 6 to 8 min. or until chicken is done, stirring frequently. Add peas, pepper and garlic; cook and stir 1 min. Remove from heat; cover to keep warm.

2   MELT butter in medium saucepan on medium heat. Stir in flour until well blended. Gradually stir in milk. Bring to boil; cook 2 min. or until thickened, stirring constantly. Add cream cheese and Romano; cook 1 to 2 min. or until cream cheese is completely melted and sauce is well blended, stirring constantly.

3   DRAIN pasta; place in large bowl. Add chicken mixture; mix lightly. Top with sauce and parsley.

Pork Medallions with Creamy Pan Sauce

Preparation time:
10 minutes

Total time:
29 minutes

Makes:
4 servings

2 tsp. oil

1 lb. pork tenderloin, cut into ½-inch-thick slices

½ cup dry white wine

1 small red pepper, chopped

1 clove garlic, minced

4 oz. (½ of 8-oz. pkg.) PHILADELPHIA Cream Cheese, cubed

1 Tbsp. chopped fresh parsley

1 HEAT oil in large skillet on medium heat. Add meat; cook 4 to 5 min. on each side or until done. Remove to serving plate; cover to keep warm.

2 ADD wine, peppers and garlic to skillet; cook and stir 2 to 3 min. or until crisp-tender. Add cream cheese; cook 4 to 5 min. or until cream cheese is melted and sauce is slightly thickened, stirring constantly.

3 SERVE sauce over meat; sprinkle with parsley.

TIP
Substitute chicken broth for the wine.

Parmesan-Crusted Chicken Supreme

Preparation time:
15 minutes

Total time:
30 minutes

Makes:
4 servings

2 cups instant brown rice, uncooked

1 can (14 oz.) fat-free reduced-sodium chicken broth, divided

6 round butter crackers, finely crushed

2 Tbsp. grated Parmesan cheese

4 small boneless skinless chicken breast halves (1 lb.)

2 tsp. oil

⅓ cup PHILADELPHIA Chive & Onion
⅓ Less Fat than Cream Cheese

¾ lb. asparagus spears, trimmed, steamed

1   COOK rice as directed on package, using 1¼ cups of the broth and ½ cup water.

2   MEANWHILE, mix cracker crumbs and Parmesan on plate. Rinse chicken with cold water; gently shake off excess. Dip chicken in crumb mixture, turning to evenly coat both sides of each breast. Discard any remaining crumb mixture.

3   HEAT oil in large nonstick skillet on medium heat. Add chicken; cook 5 to 6 min. on each side or until done (165°F). Transfer to plate; cover to keep warm. Add remaining broth and reduced-fat cream cheese to skillet; bring just to boil, stirring constantly. Cook 3 min. or until thickened, stirring frequently; spoon over chicken. Serve with rice and asparagus.

Mediterranean Meatballs with Couscous

Preparation time:
15 minutes

Total time:
37 minutes

Makes:
4 servings

1 lb. ground pork

1½ cups dry bread crumbs

½ cup (½ of 8-oz. tub) PHILADELPHIA Cream Cheese Spread

½ cup finely chopped onions

½ cup stuffed green olives, finely chopped

1 egg

2 cloves garlic, minced

1 tsp. dried oregano leaves

2 Tbsp. olive oil

1 jar (24 oz.) marinara sauce

3 cups hot cooked couscous

1   MIX first 8 ingredients until well blended; shape into 24 balls, using about 2 Tbsp. for each.

2   HEAT oil in large nonstick skillet on medium heat. Add meatballs; cook 5 to 6 min. or until evenly browned, turning occasionally. Add sauce; simmer on medium-low heat 10 to 15 min. or until meatballs are done (160°F).

3   SERVE over couscous.

Fiesta Chicken Enchiladas

Preparation time:
15 minutes

Total time:
35 minutes

Makes:
4 servings

1 small onion, chopped

1 clove garlic, minced

1 lb. cooked boneless skinless chicken breasts, shredded

1 cup salsa, divided

4 oz. (½ of 8-oz. pkg.) PHILADELPHIA Cream Cheese, cubed

1 Tbsp. chopped cilantro

1 tsp. ground cumin

1 cup shredded Cheddar & Monterey Jack cheese, divided

8 flour tortillas (6 inch)

1   HEAT oven to 350°F.

2   HEAT large skillet sprayed with cooking spray on medium heat. Add onions and garlic; cook and stir 2 min. Add chicken, ¼ cup salsa, cream cheese, cilantro and cumin; mix well. Cook 5 min. or until heated through, stirring occasionally. Add ½ cup shredded cheese; mix well.

3   SPOON about ⅓ cup chicken mixture down center of each tortilla; roll up. Place, seam-sides down, in 13x9-inch baking dish sprayed with cooking spray; top with remaining shredded cheese and salsa.

4   BAKE 15 to 20 min. or until heated through.

Thai Curry-Chicken and Rice

Preparation time:
15 minutes

Total time:
35 minutes

Makes:
4 servings, about 1½ cups each

1 Tbsp. canola oil

2 Tbsp. green curry paste

1 lb. boneless skinless chicken breasts, cut into bite-size pieces

1 small onion, thinly sliced

1 *each* red and green pepper, cut into thin strips,
    then cut crosswise in half

4 oz. (½ of 8-oz. pkg.) PHILADELPHIA ⅓ Less Fat than Cream Cheese,
    cubed

¼ cup milk

⅛ tsp. white pepper

2 cups hot cooked long-grain white rice

1   HEAT oil in large nonstick skillet on medium heat. Stir in curry paste until well blended. Add chicken and onions; cook and stir 6 to 8 min. or until chicken is done (165°F). Stir in red and green peppers; cook 4 to 5 min. or until crisp-tender, stirring frequently.

2   ADD reduced-fat cream cheese, milk and white pepper; cook until cream cheese is melted and evenly coats chicken and vegetables, stirring frequently.

3   SERVE over rice.

Roasted Veggie-Stuffed Focaccia

Preparation time:
5 minutes

Total time:
11 minutes

Makes:
2 servings

1 red pepper, halved

2 slices red onion (¼ inch thick)

4 slices *each* yellow squash and zucchini (¼ inch thick)

¼ tsp. black pepper

2 squares focaccia bread (3 inch each), cut horizontally in half

¼ cup PHILADELPHIA Spinach & Artichoke Cream Cheese Spread

1 HEAT oven to 400°F.

2 MAKE 2 or 3 small cuts in each short end of red pepper; press pepper to flatten. Spread red peppers and remaining vegetables into single layer on baking sheet sprayed with cooking spray. Sprinkle with black pepper.

3 BAKE 5 to 6 min. or until crisp-tender.

4 SPREAD cut sides of focaccia with cream cheese spread; fill with vegetables.

Creamy Lemon-Shrimp Pasta

Preparation time:
20 minutes

Total time:
20 minutes

Makes:
6 servings,
about 1¼ cups each

2 cups penne pasta, uncooked

1½ lb. uncooked deveined peeled medium shrimp

½ cup chicken broth

6 oz. (¾ of 8-oz. pkg.) PHILADELPHIA Cream Cheese, cubed

2 tsp. zest and 1 Tbsp. juice from 1 lemon

¼ cup grated Parmesan cheese

½ cup shredded mozzarella cheese

1 Tbsp. chopped fresh parsley

1 COOK pasta in large saucepan as directed on package, adding shrimp to the boiling water for the last 3 min. Meanwhile, heat broth in large skillet on medium heat. Add cream cheese, zest and juice; cook and stir 3 to 4 min. or until cream cheese is melted.

2 DRAIN pasta mixture. Add to cream cheese sauce in skillet with Parmesan; mix well.

3 TOP with mozzarella; cover. Cook 3 to 4 min. or until mozzarella is melted. Sprinkle with parsley.

Sweet Corn-Stuffed Zucchini

Preparation time:
10 minutes

Total time:
14 minutes

Makes:
4 servings

4 zucchini (1¾ lb.), parboiled

½ cup (½ of 8-oz. tub) PHILADELPHIA Chive & Onion
⅓ Less Fat than Cream Cheese

¾ cup frozen corn

½ cup chopped ham

¼ tsp. ground black pepper

1 HEAT broiler.

2 CUT zucchini lengthwise in half; scoop out centers, leaving ¼-inch-thick shells.

3 COMBINE remaining ingredients; spoon into shells.

4 BROIL, 6 inches from heat, 3 to 4 min. or until heated through and lightly browned.

TIP
To parboil zucchini, cook
4 to 5 min. in unsalted boiling
water until crisp-tender.

71

Creamy Tomato-Basil Pasta

Preparation time:
30 minutes

Total time:
30 minutes

Makes:
4 servings

3 cups penne pasta, uncooked

¼ cup sun-dried tomato dressing, divided

4 small boneless skinless chicken breasts (1 lb.)

1 cup fat-free reduced-sodium chicken broth

½ tsp. *each* garlic powder and black pepper

4 oz. (½ of 8-oz. pkg.) PHILADELPHIA ⅓ Less Fat than Cream Cheese, cubed

2 cups grape tomatoes

½ cup shredded Parmesan cheese

8 fresh basil leaves, cut into strips

1 COOK pasta as directed on package. Meanwhile, heat 2 Tbsp. dressing in large skillet on medium heat. Add chicken; cover. Cook 5 to 6 min. on each side or until done (165°F). Remove chicken from skillet; cover to keep warm. Carefully wipe out skillet with paper towel.

2 ADD remaining dressing, broth and seasonings to skillet; cook 3 to 4 min. or until heated through, stirring occasionally. Add reduced-fat cream cheese; cook and stir 2 to 3 min. or until melted. Stir in tomatoes; cook 3 min.

3 DRAIN pasta. Add to ingredients in skillet with Parmesan and basil; mix well. Serve topped with chicken.

Herbed Cream Cheese-Stuffed Lamb Burger

Preparation time:
30 minutes

Total time:
55 minutes

Makes:
4 servings

4 oz. (½ of 8-oz. pkg.) PHILADELPHIA Cream Cheese, softened

1 Tbsp. *each* chopped fresh chives and parsley

1½ lb. ground lamb

1 Tbsp. Worcestershire sauce

1 tsp. salt

½ tsp. pepper

1 Tbsp. olive oil

1 bunch watercress, thick stems removed, separated into
 equal portions

4 onion sandwich rolls, split, toasted

1   MIX cream cheese and herbs until well blended. Roll into 4 balls; flatten each into disk on sheet of waxed paper. Refrigerate 15 min. or until firm.

2   COMBINE meat, Worcestershire sauce, salt and pepper. Shape into 8 thin patties. Place cream cheese disks on 4 patties; cover with remaining patties. Press edges together to seal.

3   HEAT oil in large skillet on medium heat. Add patties; cook 5 to 6 min. on each side or until done (160°F). Serve in rolls with watercress.

TIP
Use the tines of a fork to
seal the edges of a patty.

Creamy Gnocchi

Preparation time:
15 minutes

Total time:
35 minutes

Makes:
4 servings

1 lb. frozen gnocchi, uncooked

4 slices bacon, chopped

½ lb. fresh crimini mushrooms, sliced

1 red onion, slivered

3 cloves garlic, minced

4 oz. (½ of 8-oz. pkg.) PHILADELPHIA ⅓ Less Fat than Cream Cheese, cubed

¾ cup chicken broth

¼ tsp. black pepper

¼ cup small fresh basil leaves

¼ cup shredded Parmesan cheese

1   COOK gnocchi as directed on package, omitting salt.

2   MEANWHILE, cook bacon in large skillet on medium-high heat 2 min. Add mushrooms, onions and garlic; cook and stir 5 to 6 min. or until vegetables are tender. Add reduced-fat cream cheese and broth; cook 2 to 3 min. or until cream cheese is melted, stirring constantly.

3   DRAIN gnocchi. Add to sauce in skillet with pepper; stir gently to evenly coat pasta. Cook 2 to 3 min. or until heated through, stirring constantly. Serve topped with basil and Parmesan.

Herb and Cheese-Stuffed Roast Chicken

Preparation time:
30 minutes

Total time:
2 hours

Makes:
6 servings

6 oz. (¾ of 8-oz. pkg.) PHILADELPHIA Cream Cheese, softened

1 Tbsp. fresh rosemary leaves

4 cloves garlic, minced, divided

½ tsp. freshly ground black pepper

1 whole roasting chicken (3 ½ lb.)

1 lemon, halved

¼ cup olive oil, divided

2 large baking potatoes (1 ½ lb.), peeled, cut into chunks

2 sweet potatoes (1 ½ lb.), peeled, cut into chunks

1 HEAT oven to 375°F.

2 MIX cream cheese, rosemary, half the garlic and pepper. Starting at neck of chicken, use handle of wooden spoon or fingers to carefully separate skin from meat of breast, thighs and legs, being careful not to tear the skin. Spoon cream cheese mixture under skin; use fingers to spread mixture out to thighs and legs. Place lemon halves in cavity of chicken. Place chicken in shallow pan. Brush with 2 Tbsp. oil.

3 TOSS potatoes with remaining oil and garlic in separate pan. Bake chicken and potatoes 1 ¼ to 1 ½ hours or until chicken is done (165°F), stirring potatoes every 30 min.

4 TRANSFER chicken to large serving dish, reserving juices in pan. Let chicken stand 10 min. Spoon potatoes around chicken. Skim fat from reserved juices in pan; discard fat. Spoon juices over chicken and potatoes.

Thai Chili Steak Salad

Preparation time:
10 minutes

Total time:
41 minutes

Makes:
6 servings

1 pkg. (8 oz.) PHILADELPHIA Cream Cheese

1 beef sirloin steak (1 lb.), ½ inch thick

1 pkg. (6 oz.) torn mixed salad greens

2 cups fresh green beans, blanched

¾ cup baby corn

1 small red onion, slivered

¼ cup sweet chili sauce

2 Tbsp. white vinegar

2 Tbsp. oil

2 Tbsp. chopped fresh mint

2 Tbsp. chopped cilantro

1 tsp. lime zest

¼ cup dry roasted unsalted peanuts

1 HEAT oven to 400°F.

2 CUT cream cheese into 10 slices; cut each slice diagonally in half.
   Place in single layer on parchment-covered baking sheet. Spray
   with cooking spray. Bake 10 min. or until golden brown. Set aside.

3 Heat broiler. Broil steak 6 to 8 min. on each side or until medium
   doneness (160°F). Let stand 5 min. Cut across the grain into thin slices.

4 COVER 6 plates with greens; top with beans, corn, onions, cream
   cheese and meat. Mix chili sauce and next 5 ingredients; drizzle over
   salads. Top with nuts.

Spaghetti a la PHILLY

Preparation time:
25 minutes

Total time:
25 minutes

Makes:
4 servings

½ lb. spaghetti, uncooked

1 lb. extra-lean ground beef

1 jar (24 oz.) spaghetti sauce

4 oz. (½ of 8-oz. pkg.) PHILADELPHIA Cream Cheese, cubed

2 Tbsp. grated Parmesan cheese

1   COOK spaghetti as directed on package.

2   MEANWHILE, brown meat in large skillet. Stir in sauce and cream cheese; cook on low heat 3 to 5 min. or until sauce is well blended and heated through, stirring frequently.

3   DRAIN spaghetti. Add to sauce; mix lightly. Place on platter; top with Parmesan. Garnish with chopped fresh parsley.

TIP

Add ½ cup each cooked onions and bell peppers to the sauce.

Mediterranean-Style Stuffed Chicken

Preparation time:
40 minutes

Total time:
1 hour 10 minutes

Makes:
4 servings

4 oz. (½ of 8-oz. pkg.) PHILADELPHIA Cream Cheese, softened

4 slices bacon, cooked, crumbled

2 Tbsp. dry bread crumbs

2 Tbsp. chopped kalamata olives

2 Tbsp. coarsely chopped slivered almonds

1 egg

1 Tbsp. plus 1 tsp. chopped fresh thyme, divided

4 small boneless skinless chicken breast halves (1 lb.)

2 tsp. oil

½ cup dry white wine

½ cup chicken broth

1 HEAT oven to 325°F.

2 COMBINE first 6 ingredients. Add 1 Tbsp. thyme; mix well. Use small sharp knife to cut pocket in thick long side of each chicken breast, being careful to not cut through to opposite side. Fill pockets with cream cheese mixture.

3 HEAT oil in large skillet on medium-high heat. Add chicken; cook 3 to 4 min. on each side or until browned on both sides. Transfer to 13x9-inch baking dish sprayed with cooking spray; cover. Reserve drippings in skillet.

4 BAKE 25 to 30 min. or until chicken is done (165°F). Meanwhile, add wine and broth to drippings in skillet; cook on medium heat 10 min. or until liquid is reduced by half, stirring frequently to scrape up browned bits from bottom of skillet. Stir in remaining thyme.

5 SLICE chicken. Serve topped with sauce.

Triple Cheese-Spinach Manicotti

Preparation time:
30 minutes

Total time:
1 hour 15 minutes

Makes:
6 servings

12 manicotti shells, uncooked

4 slices bacon, chopped

1 onion, chopped

2 cloves garlic, minced

1 lb. extra-lean ground beef

1 pkg. (8 oz.) PHILADELPHIA ⅓ Less Fat than Cream Cheese, softened

1 pkg. (10 oz.) frozen chopped spinach, thawed, squeezed dry

½ cup shredded mozzarella cheese

½ tsp. *each* dried basil and oregano leaves

1 jar (24 oz.) spaghetti sauce

½ cup water

½ cup shredded Parmesan cheese

1 HEAT oven to 350°F.

2 COOK pasta as directed on package. Meanwhile, cook bacon in large skillet on medium heat 4 to 5 min. or until crisp. Use slotted spoon to remove bacon from skillet, reserving drippings in skillet. Drain bacon on paper towels. Add onions and garlic to drippings; cook and stir 2 min. Add ground beef; cook and stir 6 to 7 min. or until no longer pink. Stir in bacon, reduced-fat cream cheese, spinach, mozzarella and herbs.

3 DRAIN shells; fill with meat mixture. Pour 1 cup sauce into bottom of 13x9-inch baking dish; top with shells. Add water to spaghetti sauce jar. Cover with lid and shake jar. Pour water over shells; cover with foil.

4 BAKE 45 min. or until heated through, uncovering after 35 min. Top with Parmesan.

Fish in Roasted Red Pepper Sauce

Preparation time:
10 minutes

Total time:
30 minutes

Makes:
4 servings

4 cod fillets (1 lb.)

¼ cup flour

¼ cup Italian dressing

½ cup sliced onions

2 oz. (¼ of 8-oz. pkg.) PHILADELPHIA Cream Cheese, softened

¼ cup roasted red peppers

¼ cup chicken broth

1 clove garlic, peeled

2 Tbsp. chopped cilantro

1   COAT both sides of fish with flour. Heat dressing in large skillet on medium-high heat. Add onions; cook and stir 5 min. or until crisp-tender. Add fish; cook 5 to 7 min. on each side or until fish flakes easily with fork.

2   MEANWHILE, blend cream cheese, red peppers, broth and garlic in blender until well blended. Pour into medium saucepan. Bring to boil on medium-high heat, stirring frequently; simmer on low 5 min., stirring occasionally.

3   SERVE fish topped with cream cheese sauce and parsley.

Slow-Cooked Beef and Wine Ragout

Preparation time:
15 minutes

Total time:
2 hours 30 minutes

Makes:
6 servings,
1 cup each

3 Tbsp. oil, divided

1 lb. pearl onions, peeled, halved

2 lb. boneless beef chuck eye roast, cut into 1½-inch cubes

1 can (6 oz.) tomato paste

2 cloves garlic, minced

2 cups beef broth

½ cup dry red wine

4 oz. (½ of 8-oz. pkg.) PHILADELPHIA Cream Cheese, cubed

¼ tsp. *each* salt and pepper

6 cups hot cooked rotini pasta

1 HEAT 1 Tbsp. oil in Dutch oven or large deep skillet on medium-high heat. Add onions; cook and stir 5 to 6 min. or until golden brown. Remove from pan.

2 HEAT remaining oil in pan. Add meat, in batches; cook 8 to 10 min. or until evenly browned, stirring frequently. Remove from pan. Add tomato paste and garlic; cook 1 min. Return meat to pan. Add broth and wine; stir. Bring to boil; cover. Simmer on medium-low heat 1½ hours, stirring occasionally. Add onions; cook 20 min., stirring occasionally.

3 REMOVE small amount of liquid from pan. Add to cream cheese in small bowl; mix well. Return to pan; cook 10 min., stirring occasionally. Serve with pasta.

Chicken Parmesan Bundles

Preparation time:
35 minutes

Total time:
1 hour 5 minutes

Makes:
6 servings

4 oz. (½ of 8-oz. pkg.) PHILADELPHIA Cream Cheese, softened

1 pkg. (10 oz.) frozen chopped spinach, thawed, well drained

1¼ cups shredded mozzarella cheese, divided

6 Tbsp. grated Parmesan cheese, divided

6 small boneless skinless chicken breast halves (1½ lb.),
   pounded to ¼-inch thickness

1 egg

10 round butter crackers, crushed (about ½ cup)

1½ cups spaghetti sauce, heated

1   HEAT oven to 375°F.

2   MIX cream cheese, spinach, 1 cup mozzarella and 3 Tbsp. Parmesan until well blended; spread onto chicken breasts. Starting at one short end of each breast, roll up chicken tightly. Secure with wooden toothpicks, if desired.

3   BEAT egg in shallow dish. Mix remaining Parmesan and cracker crumbs in separate shallow dish. Dip chicken in egg, then roll in crumb mixture to evenly coat. Place, seam-sides down, in 13x9-inch baking dish sprayed with cooking spray.

4   BAKE 30 min. or until chicken is done (165°F). Remove and discard toothpicks, if using. Serve chicken topped with spaghetti sauce and remaining mozzarella.

Bacon and Sweet Pea Risotto

Preparation time:
10 minutes

Total time:
40 minutes

Makes:
6 servings,
1 cup each

6 slices bacon, cut into 1-inch pieces

1 onion, chopped

1½ cups medium-grain white rice, uncooked

2 cloves garlic, minced

3 cans (15 oz. each) chicken broth

4 oz. (½ of 8-oz. pkg.) PHILADELPHIA Cream Cheese, cubed

1 cup frozen peas, thawed

2 Tbsp. chopped fresh parsley

¼ cup shredded Parmesan cheese, divided

1   COOK bacon in large skillet on medium-high heat 5 min. or just until bacon is crisp, stirring occasionally. Remove bacon from skillet with slotted spoon, reserving drippings in skillet. Drain bacon on paper towels. Add onions to drippings; cook 4 to 5 min. or until crisp-tender, stirring occasionally.

2   ADD rice and garlic; cook 3 min. or until rice is opaque, stirring frequently. Gradually add ½ can broth, cook and stir 3 min. or until broth is completely absorbed. Repeat with remaining broth, stirring in cream cheese with the last addition of broth and cooking 5 min. or until cream cheese is completely melted and mixture is well blended.

3   STIR in peas; cook 2 min. or until heated through, stirring occasionally. Remove from heat. Stir in bacon, parsley and 1 Tbsp. Parmesan. Serve topped with remaining Parmesan.

TIP
Substitute Arborio rice for the medium-grain white rice.

Maple-Cinnamon Baked French Toast

Preparation time:
15 minutes

Total time:
1 hour 35 minutes
(incl. refrigerating)

Makes:
8 servings

1 pkg. (8 oz.) PHILADELPHIA Cream Cheese, softened

3 eggs

1 cup milk

¼ cup maple syrup

1 tsp. vanilla

½ tsp. ground cinnamon

1 loaf Italian bread (16 oz.), cut into 16 slices

1 Tbsp. powdered sugar

1   BEAT cream cheese in medium bowl with mixer until creamy. Add next 5 ingredients; mix well.

2   DIP bread in egg mixture, turning to evenly moisten each slice; place in large shallow casserole or bowl. Add remaining egg mixture to casserole. Refrigerate 1 hour or up to 24 hours.

3   HEAT oven to 425°F. Place bread in single layer on baking sheet sprayed with cooking spray.

4   BAKE 15 to 20 min. or until golden brown, turning after 8 min. Sprinkle with sugar.

Pizza Frittata

Preparation time:
15 minutes

Total time:
30 minutes

Makes:
6 servings

6 oz. (¾ of 8-oz. pkg.) PHILADELPHIA Cream Cheese, softened

6 eggs

¼ tsp. salt

¼ tsp. *each* dried basil and oregano leaves

2 Tbsp. butter

1½ cups sliced fresh mushrooms

½ cup chopped green peppers

24 slices pepperoni, coarsely chopped

1 BEAT cream cheese, eggs, salt and seasonings until well blended.

2 MELT butter in 10-inch ovenproof skillet on medium heat. Add vegetables; cook and stir 5 min. or until crisp-tender. Stir in pepperoni and cream cheese mixture. Cover; cook 5 min. or until center is almost set.

3 HEAT broiler. Uncover frittata. Broil, 6 inches from heat, 2 to 3 min. or until golden brown.

TIP
Top each slice with
1 Tbsp. pizza sauce.

Garlic, Herb and Chili-Spiked Shrimp

Preparation time:
15 minutes

Total time:
30 minutes

Makes:
4 servings

1 Tbsp. butter

1 green onion, diagonally sliced

1 serrano chile, minced

4 cloves garlic, minced

1 lb. uncooked medium shrimp, peeled with tails left on, deveined

½ cup (½ of 8-oz. tub) PHILADELPHIA

⅓ Less Fat than Cream Cheese

½ cup chicken broth

2 cups hot cooked long-grain white rice

2 Tbsp. chopped Italian parsley

1   MELT butter in large skillet on medium heat. Add onions, chile and garlic; cook and stir 3 min. Add shrimp; cook 3 to 5 min. or until shrimp turn pink.

2   STIR in reduced-fat cream cheese and broth; simmer 5 to 6 min. or until sauce is well blended and slightly thickened, stirring constantly.

3   SPOON rice into 4 bowls; top with shrimp mixture, sauce and parsley.

TIP
Serve in spinach-lined bowl. Garnish with sliced green onions.

Smoky Spanish Chicken

Preparation time:
10 minutes

Total time:
40 minutes

Makes:
4 servings

1 Tbsp. oil

4 small boneless skinless chicken breast halves (1 lb.)

1 large onion, slivered

2 cloves garlic, minced

1 Tbsp. flour

2 tsp. smoked paprika

1 cup chicken broth

½ cup canned crushed tomatoes

½ cup (½ of 8-oz. tub) PHILADELPHIA Cream Cheese Spread

2 Tbsp. chopped fresh parsley

1   HEAT half the oil in large nonstick skillet on medium-high heat. Add chicken; cook 3 to 4 min. on each side or until browned on both sides. Remove from skillet.

2   HEAT remaining oil in skillet on medium heat. Add onions and garlic; cook and stir 5 min. or until crisp-tender. Stir in flour and paprika; cook and stir 1 min. Add broth and tomatoes. Return chicken to skillet; cover. Simmer 15 min. or until chicken is done (165°F).

3   ADD cream cheese spread; cook 2 to 3 min. or until melted, stirring frequently. Sprinkle with parsley.

Prosciutto and Basil Pizza

Preparation time:
10 minutes

Total time:
25 minutes

Makes:
6 servings

1 refrigerated ready-to-use baked pizza crust (12 inch)

¼ cup pizza sauce

½ cup (½ of 8-oz. tub) PHILADELPHIA Chive & Onion
Cream Cheese Spread

¼ lb. sliced prosciutto

12 pitted black olives

6 cherry tomatoes, halved

12 small fresh basil leaves

1 HEAT oven to 425°F.

2 SPREAD pizza crust with sauce; top with small spoonfuls of
cream cheese spread and all remaining ingredients except basil.

3 BAKE 10 to 15 min. or until crust is golden brown.

4 TOP with basil.

SIDE DISHES

Rustic Italian Bread Salad

Preparation time:
30 minutes

Total time:
30 minutes

Makes:
6 servings

4 oz. (½ of 8-oz. pkg.) PHILADELPHIA Cream Cheese, cubed

1 tsp. minced garlic, divided

1 Tbsp. lemon zest

¼ tsp. freshly ground black pepper

2 ciabatta sandwich rolls (¾ inch thick), cut horizontally in half

1 large avocado, sliced

4 cups baby arugula

1 lb. grape tomatoes, coarsely chopped

¼ cup balsamic vinegar

¼ cup olive oil

½ tsp. sugar

1 HEAT oven to 400°F.

2 PLACE cream cheese on parchment-covered baking sheet. Spray with cooking spray; sprinkle with ½ tsp. garlic, zest and pepper. Bake 8 to 10 min. until lightly browned. Cool slightly.

3 MEANWHILE, cut each bread piece diagonally in half; place on baking sheet. Spray with cooking spray. Bake 3 to 5 min. on each side or until golden brown on both sides.

4 ARRANGE toast slices and avocados on platter; top with arugula, tomatoes and cream cheese. Beat vinegar, oil, sugar and remaining garlic with whisk until well blended. Drizzle over salad.

Roasted Sweet Potato and Carrot Puree

Preparation time:
15 minutes

Total time:
1 hour 20 minutes

Makes:
6 servings,
⅔ cup each

1 lb. sweet potatoes (about 3), peeled, cut into ½-inch pieces

1 lb. carrots (about 8), peeled, cut into ½-inch slices

3 Tbsp. olive oil

2 Tbsp. brown sugar

1 tsp. salt

1½ cups chicken broth, divided

4 oz. (½ of 8-oz. pkg.) PHILADELPHIA ⅓ Less Fat than Cream Cheese, cubed

1 HEAT oven to 375°F.

2 COMBINE first 5 ingredients; spread onto bottom of 15x10x1-inch pan. Pour 1 cup broth over vegetable mixture.

3 BAKE 45 to 55 min. or until broth is absorbed and vegetables are tender and caramelized, stirring occasionally.

4 SPOON vegetables into food processor. Add remaining broth and reduced-fat cream cheese; process until smooth. Return to pan; cook 10 min. or until heated through, stirring frequently.

TIP
Roast additional vegetables to add texture and a garnish to this side dish.

New Potatoes in Dill Cream Sauce

Preparation time:
10 minutes

Total time:
30 minutes

Makes:
16 servings,
about ½ cup each

2 ½ lb. new potatoes, quartered

1 tub (8 oz.) PHILADELPHIA Chive & Onion Cream Cheese Spread

¼ cup milk

1 green pepper, chopped

3 Tbsp. chopped fresh dill

1   COOK potatoes in boiling water in saucepan on medium heat 15 min. or until potatoes are tender; drain.

2   MEANWHILE, microwave cream cheese spread, milk and peppers in large microwaveable bowl on HIGH 40 to 50 sec. or until cream cheese spread is melted when stirred. Stir in dill until well blended.

3   ADD potatoes; toss to coat.

TIP
Chill and serve as a cold potato salad, stirring in a small amount of additional milk to thin if necessary.

Saucy Ribbon Vegetables

Preparation time:
15 minutes

Total time:
25 minutes

Makes:
6 servings

1 cup water

4 carrots (¾ lb.), cut lengthwise into very thin slices

2 zucchini, cut lengthwise into very thin slices

½ cup (½ of 8-oz. tub) PHILADELPHIA Chive & Onion
⅓ Less Fat than Cream Cheese

¼ tsp. salt

⅛ tsp. freshly ground black pepper

1   BRING water to boil in medium saucepan on medium-high heat. Add carrots; cover. Cook 1 min. Add zucchini; cook, covered, 3 min. Use slotted spoon to transfer vegetables to bowl; reserve water in pan.

2   WHISK reduced-fat cream cheese into reserved water; cook on medium heat 2 to 3 min. or until sauce is well blended, whisking constantly.

3   SPOON vegetables onto platter; top with sauce.

TIP
Try yellow squash instead
of the carrots or zucchini.

Creamy Spinach

Preparation time:
5 minutes

Total time:
18 minutes

Makes:
4 servings,
about ⅔ cup each

1 tsp. olive oil

½ cup sliced red onions

4 oz. (½ of 8-oz. pkg.) PHILADELPHIA ⅓ Less Fat than Cream Cheese,
   cubed

1 Tbsp. fat-free milk

¼ tsp. *each* salt and pepper

2 pkg. (6 oz. each) baby spinach leaves

1 HEAT oil in medium saucepan on medium-high heat. Add onions; cook
   and stir 3 to 4 min. or until crisp-tender.

2 STIR in reduced-fat cream cheese, milk and seasonings; cook on low
   heat 1 to 2 min. or until cream cheese is melted and sauce is well blended.

3 ADD ⅓ of the spinach; cook 2 min. or just until wilted, stirring frequently.
   Add remaining spinach in batches, cooking and stirring 1 to 2 min. after
   each addition.

TIP

Try this with Swiss chard
instead of the spinach.

Spinach-Artichoke Mashed Potatoes

Preparation time:
10 minutes

Total time:
30 minutes

Makes:
8 servings,
about ½ cup each

2 ½ lb. baking potatoes (about 7), peeled, quartered

1 tub (8 oz.) PHILADELPHIA Spinach & Artichoke
  Cream Cheese Spread

1 Tbsp. butter or margarine

1 tsp. salt

1 COOK potatoes in boiling water in large saucepan 20 min. or until tender; drain.

2 MASH potatoes until smooth.

3 STIR in remaining ingredients until well blended.

TIP
Prepare using PHILADELPHIA
Chive & Onion Cream Cheese Spread.

Lemon-Parsley Baby Carrots

Preparation time:
5 minutes

Total time:
35 minutes

Makes:
4 servings,
about ⅔ cup each

1 lb. baby carrots

1 cup water

⅓ cup chicken broth

4 oz. (½ of 8-oz. pkg.) PHILADELPHIA ⅓ Less Fat than Cream Cheese, cubed

1 tsp. lemon zest

1 Tbsp. chopped fresh parsley

1 BRING carrots and water to boil in medium saucepan on medium-high heat; cover. Cook 6 to 8 min. or until carrots are crisp-tender. Use slotted spoon to transfer carrots to bowl; reserve water in pan.

2 RETURN water to boil; cook 6 to 8 min. or until water is reduced by half. Add broth, reduced-fat cream cheese and zest; stir. Simmer on low heat 2 to 3 min. or until cream cheese is melted and sauce is well blended, stirring frequently. Stir in parsley.

3 ADD carrots; toss to coat.

TIP
This sauce is also great served over broccoli spears.

Creamy Corn and Turkey Soup

Preparation time:
10 minutes

Total time:
25 minutes

Makes:
6 servings,
1 cup each

½ cup chopped onions

1 red pepper, chopped, divided

2 Tbsp. butter or margarine

4 oz. (½ of 8-oz. pkg.) PHILADELPHIA Cream Cheese, cubed

2 cups shredded cooked turkey

1 can (14.75 oz.) cream-style corn

2 cups chicken broth

¾ cup milk

½ tsp. cracked black pepper

1 COOK onions and half the peppers in butter in large saucepan on medium heat 5 to 6 min. or until crisp-tender, stirring frequently.

2 ADD cream cheese; cook on low heat 3 to 4 min. or until melted, stirring constantly. Stir in turkey, corn, broth and milk.

3 COOK 5 min. or until soup is heated through, stirring occasionally. Serve topped with remaining red peppers and black pepper.

Simple Cheese Soufflé

Preparation time:
15 minutes

Total time:
1 hour

Makes:
4 servings

6 eggs, separated

1 pkg. (8 oz.) PHILADELPHIA Cream Cheese, cubed, softened

1 tsp. *each* chopped fresh basil, oregano and thyme

⅛ tsp. salt

1   HEAT oven to 350°F.

2   BLEND 3 egg whites in blender 2 min. or until frothy; pour into medium bowl.

3   ADD remaining yolks, whole eggs and all remaining ingredients to blender; blend well. Add to beaten egg whites; stir gently until well blended. Pour into 4 (1-cup) ramekins sprayed with cooking spray.

4   BAKE 30 to 35 min. or until centers are set and tops are puffed and lightly browned. Serve immediately.

TIP

For added flavor, prepare using PHILADELPHIA Chive & Onion Cream Cheese Spread.

Creamy Citrus-Chive Asparagus

Preparation time:
15 minutes

Total time:
15 minutes

Makes:
6 servings

2 lb. fresh asparagus spears, trimmed

1 Tbsp. water

¼ cup fat-free reduced-sodium chicken broth

½ cup (½ of 8-oz. tub) PHILADELPHIA Chive & Onion
    Cream Cheese Spread

½ tsp. lemon zest

1   PLACE asparagus in microwaveable casserole. Add water; cover with waxed paper. Microwave on HIGH 4 to 5 min. or until asparagus is crisp-tender.

2   MEANWHILE, heat broth in small saucepan. Add cream cheese spread; cook until cream cheese is melted and sauce is slightly thickened, stirring constantly.

3   DRAIN asparagus; top with sauce and zest.

TIP
Divide cooked asparagus spears into 6 bundles and tie each with a steamed green onion for a simple and elegant presentation.

Oat-Topped Sweet Potato Crisp

Preparation time:
20 minutes

Total time:
60 minutes

Makes:
8 servings

1 pkg. (8 oz.) PHILADELPHIA Cream Cheese, softened

1 can (40 oz.) cut sweet potatoes, drained

¾ cup packed brown sugar, divided

¼ tsp. ground cinnamon

1 Granny Smith apple, chopped

⅔ cup chopped cranberries

½ cup flour

½ cup old-fashioned or quick-cooking oats, uncooked

⅓ cup cold butter or margarine

¼ cup chopped pecans

1   HEAT oven to 350°F.

2   BEAT cream cheese, potatoes, ¼ cup sugar and cinnamon with mixer until well blended. Spoon into 1½-qt. casserole; top with apple and cranberries.

3   MIX flour, oats and remaining sugar in medium bowl; cut in butter until mixture resembles coarse crumbs. Stir in nuts. Sprinkle over fruit layer in casserole.

4   BAKE 35 to 40 min. or until heated through.

DESSERTS

Dark Chocolate-Hazelnut Soufflé

Preparation time:
10 minutes

Total time:
55 minutes

Makes:
6 servings

1 tsp. butter

½ cup plus 1 Tbsp. sugar

6 eggs

1 tub (8 oz.) PHILADELPHIA Cream Cheese Spread

1 Tbsp. hazelnut-flavored liqueur

3 oz. bittersweet chocolate, melted

2 Tbsp. hazelnuts, toasted, chopped

1 HEAT oven to 350°F.

2 GREASE bottom and side of 1-qt. soufflé dish or casserole with butter; sprinkle with 1 Tbsp. sugar.

3 BLEND eggs, cream cheese spread, remaining sugar, liqueur and chocolate in blender 30 sec. or until smooth. Blend on high speed 15 sec. Pour into soufflé dish.

4 BAKE 40 to 45 min. or until puffed. Top with nuts. Serve immediately.

TIP
Serve topped with
mixed berries.

Almond-Pear Cream Cheese Torte

Preparation time:
30 minutes

Total time:
4 hours 5 minutes
(incl. refrigerating)

Makes:
12 servings

½ cup butter or margarine, softened

1 cup sugar, divided

1 cup flour

1 pkg. (8 oz.) PHILADELPHIA Cream Cheese, softened

1 egg

½ tsp. vanilla

½ tsp. ground cinnamon

4 fresh pears (1¼ lb.), peeled, sliced

¼ cup sliced almonds

1   HEAT oven to 425°F.

2   BEAT butter and ⅓ cup sugar in small bowl with mixer until light and fluffy. Add flour; mix well. Press onto bottom and 1 inch up side of 9-inch springform pan.

3   BEAT cream cheese and ⅓ cup of the remaining sugar in same bowl with mixer until well blended. Add egg and vanilla; mix well. Spread onto bottom of crust. Mix remaining sugar and cinnamon. Add to pears in large bowl; toss to coat. Arrange over cream cheese layer; top with nuts. Bake 10 min.

4   REDUCE temperature to 375°F; bake torte 25 min. or until center is set. Cool completely. Run knife around rim of pan to loosen torte. Remove rim. Refrigerate torte 3 hours.

New York Cheesecake

Preparation time:
15 minutes

Total time:
5 hours 25 minutes
(incl. refrigerating)

Makes:
16 servings

6 honey graham crackers, crushed (about 1 cup)

3 Tbsp. sugar

3 Tbsp. butter or margarine, melted

5 pkg. (8 oz. each) PHILADELPHIA Cream Cheese, softened

1 cup sugar

3 Tbsp. flour

1 Tbsp. vanilla

1 cup sour cream

4 eggs

1 can (21 oz.) cherry pie filling

1 HEAT oven to 325°F.

2 LINE 13x9-inch pan with foil, with ends of foil extending over sides. Mix graham crumbs, 3 Tbsp. sugar and butter; press onto bottom of pan. Bake 10 min.

3 MEANWHILE, beat cream cheese, 1 cup sugar, flour and vanilla with mixer until well blended. Add sour cream; mix well. Add eggs, 1 at a time, mixing on low after each just until blended. Pour over crust.

4 BAKE 40 min. or until center is almost set. Cool completely. Refrigerate 4 hours. Use foil handles to lift cheesecake from pan before cutting to serve. Top with pie filling.

Delicate Peaches-and-Cream Napoleons

Preparation time:
25 minutes

Total time:
25 minutes
(plus cooling)

Makes:
6 servings

4 sheets frozen phyllo dough

2 Tbsp. brown sugar, divided

1 tsp. vanilla

1 can (14 oz.) peach slices in juice, well drained

1 tub (8 oz.) PHILADELPHIA ⅓ Less Fat than Cream Cheese

1 Tbsp. powdered sugar

1 HEAT oven to 375°F.

2 STACK phyllo sheets, spraying each with cooking spray before covering with another sheet; spray top with cooking spray. Cut stack into 12 rectangles. Place, 2 inches apart, on parchment-covered baking sheet. Bake 2 min. or until crisp and golden brown; cool.

3 MEANWHILE, cook and stir 1 Tbsp. brown sugar and vanilla in large nonstick skillet on low heat 1 to 2 min. or until sugar is melted. Add peaches; cook and stir 1 min. or until evenly coated with sugar mixture. Cool.

4 MIX reduced-fat cream cheese and remaining brown sugar until well blended. Top 6 phyllo rectangles with cream cheese mixture and peach mixture; cover with remaining phyllo rectangles. Sprinkle with powdered sugar. Serve immediately.

Red Velvet Cupcakes

Preparation time:
15 minutes

Total time:
1 hour 10 minutes
(incl. cooling)

Makes:
24 servings

1 pkg. (2-layer size) red velvet cake mix

1 pkg. (3.9 oz.) chocolate instant pudding

1 pkg. (8 oz.) PHILADELPHIA Cream Cheese, softened

½ cup butter or margarine, softened

1 pkg. (16 oz.) powdered sugar (about 4 cups)

1 cup thawed frozen whipped topping

1 square (1 oz.) white chocolate, shaved into curls

1 PREPARE cake batter and bake as directed on package for 24 cupcakes, blending dry pudding mix into batter before spooning into prepared muffin cups. Cool.

2 MEANWHILE, beat cream cheese and butter in large bowl with mixer until well blended. Gradually beat in sugar. Whisk in whipped topping. Spoon 1½ cups into small freezer-weight resealable plastic bag; seal bag. Cut small corner off bottom of bag. Insert tip of bag into top of each cupcake to pipe about 1 Tbsp. frosting into center of cupcake.

3 FROST cupcakes with remaining frosting. Top with chocolate curls. Keep refrigerated.

TIP

To make chocolate curls, first warm an unwrapped square in the microwave on HIGH for a few seconds. Then draw a peeler slowly across square's bottom for long curls and across the narrow side for short curls.

White Chocolate-Raspberry Cake

Preparation time:
30 minutes

Total time:
1 hour 28 minutes
(incl. cooling)

Makes:
16 servings

2 pkg. (6 squares each) white chocolate, divided

¾ cup butter or margarine, softened, divided

1 pkg. (2-layer size) white cake mix

1 cup milk

3 eggs

2 tsp. vanilla, divided

1 pkg. (8 oz.) PHILADELPHIA Cream Cheese, softened

2 cups powdered sugar

2 Tbsp. seedless raspberry jam

1 cup fresh raspberries

1 HEAT oven to 350°F.

2 GREASE and flour 2 (9-inch) round pans. Chop half the chocolate; place in medium microwaveable bowl. Add ½ cup butter. Microwave on HIGH 2 min. or until butter is melted. Stir until chocolate is completely melted; cool.

3 BEAT cake mix, milk, eggs, 1 tsp. vanilla and melted chocolate mixture in large bowl with mixer until well blended. Pour into prepared pans.

4 BAKE 25 to 28 min. or until toothpick inserted in centers comes out clean. Cool cakes in pans 10 min.; remove from pans to wire racks. Cool completely.

5 MELT remaining chocolate squares as directed on package. Beat cream cheese and remaining butter in large bowl with mixer until well blended. Add melted chocolate and remaining vanilla; mix well. Gradually beat in sugar until light and fluffy.

6 PLACE 1 cake layer on plate; spread with ⅔ cup frosting, then jam. Cover with remaining cake layer. Spread top and side with remaining frosting. Top with raspberries just before serving.

Strawberry Cheesecake Ice Cream

Preparation time:
20 minutes

Total time:
20 minutes
(plus freezing)

Makes:
8 servings,
about ½ cup each

1 pkg. (8 oz.) PHILADELPHIA Cream Cheese, softened

1 can (14 oz.) sweetened condensed milk

⅓ cup whipping cream

2 tsp. lemon zest

1½ cups fresh strawberries, hulled

3 honey graham crackers, coarsely chopped

1   MIX first 4 ingredients with mixer until well blended. Freeze 4 hours or until almost solid.

2   BEAT cream cheese mixture with mixer until creamy. Blend berries in blender until smooth. Add to cream cheese mixture with chopped grahams; mix well. Freeze 8 hours or until firm.

3   REMOVE dessert from freezer 15 min. before serving; let stand at room temperature to soften slightly before scooping into dishes.

TIP
Prepare using fresh or
thawed frozen blueberries.

White Chocolate-Hazelnut Cheese Balls

Preparation time:
10 minutes

Total time:
10 minutes
(plus refrigerating)

Makes:
14 servings,
2 Tbsp. each

1 pkg. (8 oz.) PHILADELPHIA Cream Cheese, softened

3 ½ oz. white chocolate, melted, cooled

1 Tbsp. sugar

½ cup hazelnuts, toasted, chopped

1 MIX first 3 ingredients until well blended.

2 REFRIGERATE 1 hour or until firm enough to handle.

3 SHAPE into 2 balls; coat with nuts.

TIP

For truffles, mix ingredients and refrigerate as directed. Roll into 1-inch balls; coat with nuts and refrigerate until ready to serve.

Berry Clafoutis

Preparation time:
15 minutes

Total time:
35 minutes

Makes:
4 servings

½ cup plus 4 tsp. caster sugar, divided

2 cups fresh raspberries

½ cup (½ of 8-oz. tub) PHILADELPHIA Cream Cheese Spread

¼ cup flour

1 tsp. vanilla

3 eggs

½ cup milk

1 Tbsp. powdered sugar

1   HEAT oven to 400°F.

2   SPRAY 4 (1-cup) shallow ovenproof dishes with cooking spray. Sprinkle each with 1 tsp. caster sugar. Add berries.

3   BEAT cream cheese spread, remaining caster sugar, flour, vanilla and 1 egg until well blended. Add remaining eggs; mix well. Gradually beat in milk; pour over berries.

4   BAKE 20 min. or until tops are golden brown and toothpick inserted in centers of topping comes out clean. Cool slightly. Sprinkle with powdered sugar.

TIP

Caster sugar is a quick-dissolving fine sugar with a texture that is not as fine as that of powdered sugar. If you cannot find caster sugar, you can make your own by processing granulated sugar in a food processor or coffee bean grinder.

Double-Chocolate Cheesecake

Preparation time:
30 minutes

Total time:
6 hours 30 minutes
(incl. refrigerating)

Makes:
16 servings

18 cream-filled chocolate sandwich cookies, crushed

  (about 1½ cups)

2 Tbsp. butter or margarine, melted

4 pkg. (8 oz. each) PHILADELPHIA Cream Cheese, softened

1 cup granulated sugar

2 Tbsp. flour

1 tsp. vanilla

8 oz. semi-sweet chocolate, melted, cooled slightly

4 eggs

½ cup blueberries

1 Tbsp. powdered sugar

1   HEAT oven to 325°F.

2   MIX cookie crumbs and butter; press onto bottom of 9-inch springform pan. Bake 10 min.

3   BEAT cream cheese, granulated sugar, flour and vanilla with mixer until well blended. Add melted chocolate; mix well. Add eggs, 1 at a time, mixing on low speed after each just until blended. Pour over crust.

4   BAKE 55 min. to 1 hour or until center is almost set. Run knife around rim of pan to loosen cake; cool before removing rim. Refrigerate 4 hours. Top with berries just before serving; sprinkle with powdered sugar.

Espresso and Vanilla Panna Cotta

Preparation time:
30 minutes

Total time:
30 minutes
(plus refrigerating)

Makes:
8 servings

1 tsp. unflavored gelatine

1 Tbsp. boiling water

1 cup whipping cream

½ cup sugar, divided

½ vanilla bean, split

¼ cup espresso or strong black coffee

1 pkg. (8 oz.) PHILADELPHIA Cream Cheese, softened

1 DISSOLVE gelatine in boiling water; set aside. Cook cream, ¼ cup sugar and vanilla bean in small saucepan just until mixture comes to boil, stirring constantly. Remove from heat; cool.

2 MEANWHILE, cook and stir espresso and remaining sugar in separate saucepan on medium-high heat 2 to 3 min. or until sugar is dissolved; simmer on medium-low heat 2 to 3 min. or until thickened to syrup-like consistency. Pour into 8 (½-cup) espresso cups.

3 BEAT cream cheese in small bowl with mixer until creamy. Discard vanilla bean from cream mixture; gradually add to cream cheese, beating well after each addition. Blend in gelatine. Refrigerate 20 to 30 min. or until thickened but not set. Spoon into espresso cups. Refrigerate 2 hours or until firm.

Banana Split Cake

Preparation time:
15 minutes

Total time:
15 minutes
(plus refrigerating)

Makes:
24 servings

9 honey graham crackers, crushed (about 1½ cups)

1 cup sugar, divided

⅓ cup butter, melted

2 pkg. (8 oz. each) PHILADELPHIA Cream Cheese, softened

1 can (20 oz.) crushed pineapple, in juice, drained

6 bananas, divided

2 pkg. (3.4 oz. each) vanilla flavor instant pudding

2 cups cold milk

2 cups thawed frozen whipped topping, divided

1 square (1 oz.) bittersweet chocolate, shaved into curls

1   MIX crumbs, ¼ cup sugar and butter; press onto bottom of 13x9-inch pan. Freeze 10 min.

2   BEAT cream cheese and remaining sugar with mixer until well blended. Spread carefully over crust; top with pineapple. Slice 4 bananas; arrange over pineapple.

3   BEAT pudding mixes and milk with whisk 2 min. Stir in 1 cup whipped topping; spread over banana layer in pan. Top with remaining whipped topping. Refrigerate 5 hours. Slice remaining 2 bananas just before serving; arrange over dessert. Top with chocolate curls.

TIP

For tips on how to make chocolate curls, see the Red Velvet Cupcake recipe in this section.

APPENDIX

Handy Tips

How to soften cream cheese

- Place completely unwrapped package of cream cheese in microwaveable bowl.

- Microwave on HIGH 10 sec. or just until softened.

- Add 15 sec. for each additional package of cream cheese.

How to measure cream cheese

- PHILLY Brick: each package has markings in ounce increments on the foil wrapper for easy measurement, but you can also use a measuring cup to measure softened cream cheese.

- PHILLY Tub: each 8-oz. tub yields about 1 cup of cream cheese spread.

How to store cream cheese and cream cheese-frosted cakes

- Always store in refrigerator. For bricks that have been opened, rewrap tightly in plastic wrap.

- Cakes filled and/or frosted with cream cheese icing should be stored in the refrigerator.

- Freezing is not recommended.

How to melt cream cheese

PHILLY melts! Scoop a few spoonfuls of PHILLY tub or small cubes of PHILLY brick and follow these helpful hints to melt your PHILLY into sauces, soups, casseroles, and more.

- Add a few spoonfuls of PHILLY spread (or cubes of softened PHILLY brick) to warm sauce or soup and stir or whisk until cream cheese is completely melted.

- Add ½ cup of PHILLY spread (or cubes of softened PHILLY brick) to a skillet containing ¾ to 1 cup of hot milk or broth. Stir or whisk constantly until cream cheese is melted. Add ½ cup of PHILLY spread (or cubes of softened PHILLY brick) to 3 cups of hot cooked mashed potatoes and stir until combined.

How to substitute one PHILLY for another

- PHILADELPHIA Cream Cheese Flavored Spreads add the same creamy flavorful richness to dishes as regular PHILADELPHIA Cream Cheese Spread. Try varieties like PHILADELPHIA Chive & Onion or Spinach & Artichoke Cream Cheese Spreads for a simple flavor twist.

- For all of the same great flavor and creaminess, but ⅓ less fat, PHILADELPHIA ⅓ Less Fat than Cream Cheese can easily be substituted into your favorite dishes.

- In recipes, generally 4 oz. of cubed cream cheese is about equal to ½ cup of cream cheese spread.

- It is not recommended to substitute PHILADELPHIA Cream Cheese Spreads (tub) in baked items like cheesecakes or breads.

Index

Appetizers

Asian-Style Chicken and Cashew Cakes...................32

Bacon-Cheese Crescents 10

Baked Triple-Veggie Dip 16

Chicken and Corn Quesadillas........................20

Chicken and Cranberry Bites...........................26

Creamy Guacamole..24

Greek Artichoke Dip 28

Rustic Caramelized Onion Tart......................30

Smoked Salmon Chips..18

Southwest White Chicken Pizza 12

Squash and Cherry Tomato Quiche Cups.................22

Sun-Dried Tomato and Garlic Dip...............34

Tomato and Balsamic Bruschetta 14

Entrées

Asparagus and Parmesan Tart.......................48

Bacon and Sweet Pea Risotto 94

Chicken Parmesan Bundles............................92

Creamy Chicken Penne 54

Creamy Gnocchi 76

Creamy Lemon-Shrimp Pasta.......................68

Creamy Tomato-Basil Pasta..........................72

Croque Monsieur 42

Fiesta Chicken Enchiladas 62

Fish in Roasted Red Pepper Sauce...........88

Garlic, Herb and Chili-Spiked Shrimp.......................100

Grilled Salmon with Creamy
     Pesto Sauce...50

Herb and Cheese-Stuffed Roast Chicken.................78

(Entrées cont.)

Herbed Cream Cheese-Stuffed
  Lamb Burger 74

Maple-Cinnamon Baked French Toast 96

Mediterranean Meatballs with Couscous 60

Mediterranean-Style Stuffed Chicken 84

Parmesan-Crusted Chicken Supreme 58

Pizza Frittata 98

Pork Medallions with Creamy Pan Sauce 56

Prosciutto and Basil Pizza 104

Roasted Veggie-Stuffed Focaccia 66

Sausage and Peppers Lasagna 40

Savory Mushroom Omelet 52

Slow-Cooked Beef and Wine Ragout 90

Smoky Spanish Chicken 102

Spaghetti a la PHILLY 82

Steak with Creamy Peppercorn Sauce 38

Sweet Corn-Stuffed Zucchini 70

Tandoori Chicken Kabobs 46

Thai Chili Steak Salad 80

Thai Curry-Chicken and Rice 64

Trattoria Tortellini 44

Triple Cheese-Spinach Manicotti 86

Side Dishes

Creamy Citrus-Chive Asparagus 126

Creamy Corn and Turkey Soup 122

Creamy Spinach 116

Lemon-Parsley Baby Carrots 120

New Potatoes in Dill Cream Sauce 112

(Sides Dishes cont.)

Oat-Topped Sweet Potato Crisp 128

Roasted Sweet Potato and Carrot Puree 110

Rustic Italian Bread Salad 108

Saucy Ribbon Vegetables 114

Simple Cheese Soufflé 124

Spinach-Artichoke Mashed Potatoes 118

Desserts

Almond-Pear Cream Cheese Torte 134

Banana Split Cake 154

Berry Clafoutis 148

Dark Chocolate-Hazelnut Soufflé 132

Delicate Peaches-and-Cream Napoleons 138

Double-Chocolate Cheesecake 150

Espresso and Vanilla Panna Cotta 152

New York Cheesecake 136

Red Velvet Cupcakes 140

Strawberry Cheesecake Ice Cream 144

White Chocolate-Hazelnut Cheese Balls 146

White Chocolate-Raspberry Cake 142

Appendix

Acknowledgments 162

Handy Tips 158

Index 160

Acknowledgments